YOUNG PROFILES

Mary-Kate

&

Ashley Olsen

Tamara L. Britton

ABDO Publishing Company

visit us at
www.abdopub.com

Published by ABDO Publishing Company 4940 Viking Drive, Edina, Minnesota 55435.
Copyright © 1999 by Abdo Consulting Group, Inc. International copyrights reserved in
all countries. No part of this book may be reproduced in any form without written
permission from the publisher.

Printed in the United States.

Photo credits: AP/Wide World; Shooting Star
Edited by: Paul Joseph, K.M. Brielmaier

Library of Congress Cataloging-in-Publication Data

Britton, Tamara L., 1963-
    Mary-Kate and Ashley Olsen / Tamara L. Britton.
       p. cm. -- (Young profiles)
    Includes index.
    Summary: A biography of thirteen-year-old twin sisters who began their acting
careers at the age of nine months in the television series "Full House" and who
today produce and star in their own videos, CDs, and books.
    ISBN 1-57765-351-3 (hardcover)
    ISBN 1-57765-353-X (paperback)
    1. Olsen, Ashley, 1986- Juvenile literature. 2. Olsen, Mary-Kate, 1986-
Juvenile literature. 3. Actors--United States Biography Juvenile literature. [1.
Olsen, Ashley, 1986- . 2. Olsen, Mary-Kate, 1986- . 3. Actors and actresses. 4.
Women Biography.] I. Title. II. Series.
PN2285.O36B75   1999
791.45'028'092273--dc21
   [B]   99-27235
                                             CIP

Contents

The Olsen Twins

Mary-Kate and Ashley Olsen are two of today's hottest stars. The talented twins have starred in two TV series, several movies, and have made hit videos and CDs. And they're only 13 years old!

Mary-Kate and Ashley rocketed to fame on the popular TV series *Full House*. Fans have watched these pint-sized superstars grow from babies to teenagers, and their popularity is growing as fast as they are!

Television, movies, music, and books—Mary-Kate and Ashley can do it all. And their thousands of loyal fans can't wait to see what the twins will do next.

Mary-Kate and Ashley are two of the hottest young stars in the world.

Profile of Mary-Kate

Name: Mary-Kate Olsen

Date of Birth: June 13, 1986

Place of Birth: Los Angeles, California

Parents: David and Jarnie Olsen

Siblings: Brother Trent Olsen and sister Elizabeth
    Marie Olsen

Eyes: Blue

Hair: Blonde

Hobbies: Horseback riding, swimming, gymnastics, soccer,
    and basketball

Mary-Kate and Ashley on the set of
How the West was Fun.

Profile of Ashley

Name: Ashley Fuller Olsen

Date of Birth: June 13, 1986

Place of Birth: Los Angeles, California

Parents: David and Jarnie Olsen

Siblings: Brother Trent Olsen and sister Elizabeth
  Marie Olsen

Eyes: Blue

Hair: Blonde

Hobbies: Dancing, soccer, basketball, and swimming

Opposite page: The Olsen Twins'
Mother's Day Special.

Home and Family

Mary-Kate and Ashley Olsen were born on June 13, 1986. They are twins. They are **fraternal** twins, not **identical**. Though they seem to look just alike, they don't!

The twins live in California's San Fernando Valley. Their dad David is a mortgage banker. Their mom Jarnie was a professional dancer. David and Jarnie are **divorced**. Mary-Kate and Ashley have a brother and a sister. Trent and Elizabeth have appeared in some of the twins' videos.

Mary-Kate and Ashley go to their regular school when they are not working on their hit TV series or making movies. When they are working, they study on location with a **tutor**.

Mary-Kate and Ashley are not identical twins—do you know which one is on the opposite page?

Full House

When Mary-Kate and Ashley were six months old their mother took them to an **audition**. The audition was for a television show called *Full House*. In California, labor laws **restrict** the number of hours child actors can work. So, TV shows often use twins for children's roles so kids don't have to work too much at one time.

The Olsen twins won the part on *Full House*. At the age of nine months, they began sharing the role of Michelle Tanner. The first **episode** of *Full House* ran on September 22, 1987.

Full House was about a man named Danny Tanner whose wife had died. The talented actor Bob Saget played Danny Tanner. On the show, Danny had three little girls. DJ, played by Candace Cameron, Stephanie, played by Jodie Sweetin, and Michelle, who was played by Mary-Kate and Ashley.

Opposite page: Mary-Kate and Ashley took turns playing the character Michelle Tanner.

Danny needed help around the house with his kids. So, he asked his brother-in-law Jesse Katsopolis, played by John Stamos, and friend Joey Gladstone, played by Dave Coulier, to live with him and the girls.

Good **scripts** and great acting made *Full House* a mega hit. The cute twins soon **upstaged** talented **veteran** actors Bob Saget and John Stamos. As the show's popularity grew, Mary-Kate and Ashley became well-known celebrities.

Full House was on TV for eight seasons. The last **episode** ran on May 23, 1995. America couldn't get enough of the twins. Their fans waited to see what they would do next.

Opposite page: Mary-Kate and Ashley usually shared acting duties as Michelle Tanner. In this episode, Ashley (R) played Uncle Jesse's cousin from Italy.

Pint-sized Producers

After *Full House*, Mary-Kate and Ashley formed their own production company. It is called Dualstar Entertainment. Dualstar is organized into different divisions: Dualstar Entertainment, Dualstar Publications, and Dualstar Records.

With Dualstar, the twins can produce their own projects. As producers, Mary-Kate and Ashley call all the shots. They get to do the projects that they want to do, just like they want to do them. This way, the twins can give their fans exactly what they want.

Dualstar has been a huge success. In 1997, Dualstar was the number two company for top-selling videos. Only Disney sold more videos than Mary-Kate and Ashley! The twins are not only talented entertainers, they are also skilled businesswomen!

Mary-Kate and Ashley have fun on the set of To Grandmother's House We Go.

On to New Adventures

The videos that Mary-Kate and Ashley produce have been very successful. In September 1993, *Mary-Kate and Ashley: Our First Video* went to number one on *Billboard*'s music video chart in less than three weeks. It spent 12 weeks in the number one spot.

Mary-Kate and Ashley are the youngest performers to hit quadruple platinum and number one on *Billboard*'s charts. A video or album is platinum when one million copies are sold. *Mary-Kate and Ashley: Our First Video* sold more than four million copies! It was one of the top 10 videos for 157 weeks!

The Adventures of Mary-Kate and Ashley videos are mysteries. The twins play detectives called the Trenchcoat Twins who can "solve any crime by dinner time." The videos are fun and take place in unusual locations. All of the mystery videos have been certified triple platinum by *Billboard*'s kid video chart.

The twins also make party videos. In the You're Invited to Mary-Kate and Ashley's videos, the twins have parties and the viewer is invited! The parties take place at places everyone loves to go, like the mall, the ballet, and the beach.

The hit party videos are musicals, and through Dualstar Records, Mary-Kate and Ashley release CDs and cassettes of music from their party videos. Fans can get song **lyrics** from the twins' Web site or fan club and sing along with Mary-Kate and Ashley!

Mary-Kate and Ashley's busy schedule includes being on shows like The Rosie O'Donnell Show.

Twins in Print

Through their Dualstar Publications, Mary-Kate and Ashley publish books based on their hit videos.

Adventures of Mary-Kate and Ashley and the New Adventures of Mary-Kate and Ashley series are mystery stories. Fans can follow the adventures of the Trenchcoat Twins as they solve mysteries.

There are also books based on the You're Invited to Mary-Kate and Ashley's series of party videos. The twins have recently released a series of books that go with their new TV series *Two of a Kind.*

Mary-Kate and Ashley's books are as popular with their fans as their videos and CDs! Fans can't get enough of the twins' adventures! There are millions of Mary-Kate and Ashley's books in print, and a new book is released each month.

Opposite page: The Olsen Twins in Double, Double, Toil and Trouble.

Movie Stars

In addition to their home video series, Mary-Kate and Ashley have starred in movies. *To Grandmother's House We Go* was released in 1992. It was followed by *Double, Double, Toil and Trouble* in 1993 and *How the West was Fun* in 1994. These movies were made to show on TV.

The twins moved to the big screen with their first feature film *It Takes Two* in 1995. *Billboard Dad*, a feature-length film on video, was released in 1998.

Look for a new movie, *Switching Goals*, about two soccer-playing sisters, coming soon. It will be shown on the *Wonderful World of Disney*.

Opposite page: Mary-Kate and Ashley in It Takes Two.

Two of a Kind

Mary-Kate and Ashley have a new TV series called *Two of a Kind*. It is about two twins named Mary-Kate and Ashley Burke. Mary-Kate is a tomboy who likes baseball more than school. Ashley is an excellent student who is interested in boys.

Christopher Sieber plays the Burke sisters' dad, Kevin. Kevin is a college **professor** who has hired one of his students to **supervise** Mary-Kate and Ashley while he is at work.

Sally Wheeler plays the student, Carrie. The twins' dad is not sure that Carrie is the best choice to watch the twins. But Mary-Kate and Ashley think Carrie is totally cool!

Opposite page: Mary-Kate (R) and Ashley in the hit show Two of a Kind.

A Fabulous Future

Mary-Kate and Ashley Olsen are the most popular child celebrities in the entertainment industry today. Their production company is very successful and they have a knack for picking projects that their fans will like.

On *Full House*, they were babies who shared a role. Through smart business decisions and hard work, the twins are now recognized as individual talented entertainers.

The twins have been named Teen Ambassadors to the 1999 Women's World Cup soccer tournament. With so many projects in the works and possibilities to explore, Mary-Kate and Ashley Olsen have a bright future ahead.

*Mary-Kate (L) and Ashley join the U.S. Women's World
Cup soccer team as they jump through drills.*

Fun Facts on Mary-Kate and Ashley

- Ashley is two minutes older than Mary-Kate.

- Mary-Kate is left-handed.

- Mary-Kate and Ashley once suited up with the Minnesota Twins.

- Mary-Kate and Ashley might seem exactly alike, but Ashley has a freckle on her lower lip and Mary-Kate has two freckles on her right cheek.

How to Contact the Olsen Twins

You can write to Mary-Kate and Ashley at:

Two of a Kind
Mary-Kate and Ashley Olsen
C/O Warner Brothers Studios
4000 Warner Boulevard
Burbank, CA 91522

Join Mary-Kate and Ashley's Fan Club

Mary-Kate and Ashley's Fan Club
859 Hollywood Way
Suite 275
Burbank, CA 91505

Glossary

Audition: a short performance to show ability to get a part in a TV show or movie.

Divorce: a legal act that ends a marriage.

Episode: one individual show in a TV series.

Fraternal: twins that are different from each other in some ways.

Identical: twins that are exactly alike.

Lyrics: the words to a song.

Professor: a teacher at a college or university.

Restrict: to keep within certain limits.

Script: the text or words that actors say in a TV show or a movie.

Supervise: to watch over and take care of something.

Tutor: a private teacher.

Upstage: when an actor is more popular and talented than other actors in a TV show or movie.

Veteran: a person with a lot of experience.

Olsens on the Web

Check out Mary-Kate and Ashley on the Web at the ONLY official Olsen twins site:

www.marykateandashley.com

Visit other great sites devoted to Mary-Kate and Ashley:
http://abc.go.com/tgif/two_of_a_kind/index.html
www.olsentwins.net
www.trenchcoattwins.com

Pass It On

Educate readers around the country by passing on information you've learned about your favorite young celebrity. Share your little-known facts and interesting stories. Tell others about your favorite TV shows, movies, books, and songs. We want to hear from you!

To get posted on the ABDO Publishing Company Web site, email us at "youngprofiles@abdopub.com"

Visit the ABDO Publishing Company Web site at www.abdopub.com

Index